Eli, Eli

Kathleen James

Vocamus Press
Guelph, Ontario

Copyright © 2012 Kathleen James
All rights reserved

ISBN 13: 978-0-9881049-2-1 (ebk)
ISBN 13: 978-0-9881049-0-7 (pbk)

Vocamus Press
130 Dublin Street, North
Guelph, Ontario, Canada
N1H 4N4

www.vocamus.net

2012

In memory of Eli, our son,
who taught us much about life, love, joy,
and the strength of the human spirit.

Author's Note

Eli Eli was written over thirty years ago to help me come to grips with the loss of our son Eli to cancer. It was first published in 1981 under the name Louisa Lord, my middle and maiden names. With this edition I have made some minor editorial changes, and I have decided to publish it under the name by which I am known.

The date beneath each poem is the date when it was written. Other than the first, the poems are all in chronological order.

The cover photograph was taken by a photographer who was taking pictures of new church plants for the Baptist Convention of Ontario and Quebec. When a member of our congregation saw it at the Convention's Annual Meeting, he told them of Eli's illness, and the photograph was graciously passed on to our family.

"Eli, Eli, lema sabachthani?" –
which means, "My God, my God,
why have you forsaken me?"
      Matthew 27: 46 (NIV)

Beyond Friday

It was a Friday morning when you died.
Cancer had wasted and broken your body,
But not your spirit.
For that I am thankful.

Oh, how I mourn you!
How I ache, not just with the memories of what was,
But also of what can never be.
For, my son, you knew life not quite three years.

But for most of that time you knew life as only a child can,
Joyously.

I remember how you loved to 'play' the piano, the guitar, the
        drums,
How you liked to play parade with your Daddy.
At times such memories fill me with anger as well as anguish.
Your death seems so senseless, such a waste.

Only when I remember that other Friday,
That Friday at Calvary,
Do I glimpse a ray of hope
That beyond your Friday there is also an Easter Sunday.

                              July 12, 1978

Innocent

I noticed the bump to the side of your right eye.
It seemed innocent enough,
For you were a physically active child who often sported at
    least one bump or cut.
I casually mentioned it to your father that night at supper.
Later, playing with you, Daddy found that you didn't mind if
    he touched it.

We decided to let the doctor look at it.
In the next few days, you saw several doctors, had several
    series of x-rays taken.
The diagnosis: external angular dermoid, nothing to worry
    about, easily removed.

Since your face was involved we felt that we'd prefer a plastic
    surgeon to do the surgery.
Within two weeks of us noticing the bump, the surgeon saw
    you.
His resident asked if I had noticed that your right eye was
    pushed forward slightly.
I became aware of a terror growing in me.
Yet despite my medical background, I didn't suspect what was
    the likely cause.
The surgeon was calm, reassuring, but firm.
We must admit you for further tests.

That Sunday we admitted you.
I remember you running around, laughing, exploring the
    well-stocked toy room.
The angiogram was to be Monday, but being delayed until
    Tuesday,
We got a pass for that Monday afternoon and went to your
    cousins'.
It was a beautiful day.
I watched as the four of you played and fought together.

Tuesday morning, while waiting for them to come for you,
We read your favourite books.
They came and took you away.
Grandma came and waited with me.
We read.
Then we heard you were in the recovery room lying on your
    back, kicking your blankets in the air.
It sounded just like you.

They asked when your Daddy would be coming.
The doctor wanted to speak to both of us together.

Daddy arrived.
We went with the doctor.
The angiogram results were clear.
It was a tumour!
It was large, pressing up under the brain, pushing your right
    eye forward.
It had eaten a lot of the bone.
It was a secondary.
The primary was in the adrenal gland above your right kidney.
The prognosis was dismal!

We were dazed.
How could this be?
You were so happy, so healthy, so full of life.
It was supposed to be just an innocent bump.

Walking back to your room I saw you lying asleep in the crib,
    quiet, peaceful.
I tried to grasp that within you was a force, a tumour,
    tumours, neither quiet nor peaceful.

May 3, 1979

No Escape

It was with a great feeling of relief that we took you home.
It was only for a week-end, but I had a feeling of exhilaration.
It was as if I shed at the hospital door the fact that you had
    cancer, that the prognosis was dismal.
Now we were taking you home, and all would be well.
Of course in my head I knew this wasn't true, but once free of
    the hospital my heart took over.

You had never really been 'sick' with cancer.
Only the bump at the side of your head and your bulging right
    eye witnessed to its presence.
The last three days in hospital you had not been yourself.
But then there had been the biopsy, the IVP, the anasthetic
    and the drugs necessary for these,
So we had not been alarmed.

Soon after we arrived home we had you settled in your own
    room, in your own crib.
We even started planning what we would do the next day.

But there was no escaping reality, not even for a week-end.
We hadn't even gone to bed ourselves when you began crying
    out.
For the first time we knew that you were in pain.
Through the night we learned that you were only comfortable
    sitting up,
So Daddy and I took turns sitting up cradling you against our
    chests.

The next morning we returned to London.
A different hospital, this time the Children's hospital.
A different hospital, but the same reality.
This time there was no escape.

                                September 8, 1979

It's Okay

For the first three or four days in hospital things were
 confused.
What with the week-end, a urine test not started at the right
 time of day,
A drug that stimulated rather than sedated Eli, delaying the
 start of his cobalt treatments;
There was no rhythm to his day, no predictability.
I felt adrift.
I needed something to concentrate on.

But slowly the routine developed; I had my focus.
Eli had his cobalt in the morning, his chemo in the afternoon.
He had to be sedated for his cobalt; they couldn't take the
 chance that he would move.
The treatment field was the upper right quarter of his head,
 radiated both from the front and back.

I would go with him to cobalt.
Moving him from the stretcher to the treatment table would
 wake him up.
I would soothe him by stroking his face and saying, "It's okay,
 Eli. It's okay. Mommy is here. Go back to sleep son.
 It's okay."
Outside, watching the treatment on closed circuit T.V., I'd be
 praying that he wouldn't wake up, that he wouldn't
 move.

It would take Eli three or four hours to wake up from the
 effects of the drug.
Then he'd be in a frenzy, asking for everything, not knowing
 what he wanted.
This would last several hours, then he would be himself again,
Wanting to be pulled in the wagon through the halls.

While in hospital the chemo was relatively easy since Eli had
    an I.V. running.
But oh the agony of keeping it running.
Every night his Daddy stayed in his room with him,
Watching the I.V. tubing didn't get tangled when he turned.
Holding him, talking with him when he couldn't get to sleep,
Changing his diaper.
During the day I was with him, his grandmother or his aunt
    would come when I went for meals.

After ten days Eli was discharged.
Eli and I stayed at my parents' place since his cobalt
    treatment was to continue.
At first Eli could hardly walk he was so weak,
But slowly he regained his strength.

Each morning we went over to my sister's.
Eli played in the backyard with her three children.
We'd have lunch back at Grandma's.
Then Grandma, an R.N., would give him his needle.
We would drive him to the hospital for his cobalt treatment.
Afterwards we'd have his blood tested.
Back at Grandma's he'd sleep for about three hours.
After he awoke he'd be in a frenzy for several hours.
Papa, Grandma and I would take turns taking him for a walk,
    going over to his uncle's, going for a ride in the car, or
    just being with him until this passed.

But Eli was getting stronger.
The eye was going down.
Perhaps I was right when I said, "It's okay."

                                                  September 8, 1979

A Second Time

You were admitted to hospital for testing six weeks after
    cobalt and chemo had terminated.
Your bone marrow was clear; the scan showed nothing new.
They wanted to operate to try and remove the primary.

Hope sprang up.
I wanted that surgery badly, not the surgery really, but the
    chance at life that it promised.
Your Daddy hesitated but then agreed.

Leaving you at the elevator going up to the surgical floor
Tore at me.
You weren't asleep, and you called out to us.
But we couldn't go any further.

We went and had lunch; then we waited.
Three, four hours passed.
As they passed my hope grew.
They must have been able to get the tumor or they wouldn't
    be this long, I reasoned.

Your Daddy left to go over to the operating rooms.
It wasn't ten minutes before he was back with the surgeon.
The surgeon had just finished.
He couldn't get it.
He had tried for three hours.
The tumor was too intimately involved with the major
    abdominal blood vessels.
He had tagged it.
You were to have more cobalt.

I was stunned!
The surgery that I had hoped would give you life
Only forced me to face your death a second time.

                                            September 8, 1979

Re-run

Your recovery from the surgery for the most part was
    uneventful.
We were used to the hospital and its routine.
Soon we were back to our old scheduling.
I did days, Daddy nights, and Grandma and Aunt Marilynne
    spelled me for meals.

Shortly before leaving the hospital your cobalt treatments
    started.
They knew us well in cobalt.
They were pleased to see how your eye had returned to its
    natural position.
Because your remaining perfectly still wasn't as critical when
    radiating the abdomen,
They decided you didn't need to be drugged.

At the beginning of the cobalt there were several nights that
    you were very sick to your stomach.
You were scheduled for twenty-five treatments.
I was fearful that our nightmare had taken another twist.
But soon your body seemed to adjust.
Your appetite remained poor, but you weren't sick, and you
    were able to rest well.

We were back staying at Grandma and Papa's by then.
Once again mornings found you playing with your cousins.
In the afternoon you had your cobalt and blood-work done.
But this time you were awake for your treatments.
At first you were afraid and anxious; you cried.
But by the end of the second week of treatments you were
    laughing and talking with the technicians.
Of course the candy they always gave you after your treatment
Might have had something to do with winning you over.
During this time one big thing happemed that was different,
    that was not a re-run of before:
Jaya was born; you were now a big brother.

                                September 8, 1979

Decision

We had been back in our own home about three weeks,
A family again.
Daddy going off to work,
You adjusting to your new role as a big brother to Jaya.

I called London to see what St. Jude's had advised should be
    our next step.
I was told further chemotherapy, with the same drugs that had
    seemed to fail before,
Then surgery again.
I couldn't believe it.
Daddy and I talked.
We set up a meeting with the doctors and social worker.
They agreed to our getting a second opinion.
They warned that since no one was succeeding with this type
    of cancer it was sure to be a different opinion.

You had a body scan.
Then we had a consult.
You showed no further cancer, but you weren't healing the
    bone damage.
The doctor held out little hope.
However, the drugs she advised using weren't as toxic, they
    wouldn't be as hard on you.
She also felt her program offered you as much hope as the
    other.
She said statistically it made no difference whether the
    primary was removed or not.

We wanted you not only to live but to enjoy life,
To know its joy.
We had even thought of discontinuing all treatment, since no
    treatment held out much hope.
But all the doctors discouraged this.
So after careful consideration,
We went with the Toronto drug routine, with London and
    then eventually Kitchener supervising.
Because it was less toxic it would allow you to have a more
    normal life,
And we hoped at the same time it would control the cancer.

                                        September 8, 1979

Waiting

Usually it would just be the three of us,
Jaya, you and I, that would pile in the car
Heading for Kitchener, for your chemotherapy.
There was always an excitement
About going out in the car.
From the time you were a baby, you loved it.
Feeling this excitement in you, even on these trips,
I felt somehow deceptive for I knew their purpose.
And although I told you where we were going, when you asked,
Your mood never seemed to dampen.

Even in the hall, waiting your turn,
You were full of fun, full of joy, full of curiosity.
We would watch the custodian clean the floor,
Always the same man, friendly, talkative.
We would go and investigate the mysterious noise
Of the saw, coming from the Plaster Room.
I would read to you.
You would play on the floor with your cars and trucks.
You would lean against the wall, crossing one leg over the
      other,
Then have me imitate you.
You would then run a little further down the hall,
Repeat the posture, and gesture for me to do the same.
Many were the trips we made to the water fountain.
I held you as you turned the handle and let the water flow
      through your mouth and splash your face.

These activities would be interrupted for your blood test.
As soon as you had to go into the treatment room
Your mood abruptly changed.
You became frightened, angry.
You screamed!
You struggled on my knee as I held you.
I could do nothing to comfort you.

After your thumb was pricked,
You settled right down,
Watched as they took the smear,
As they drew the blood into the fine glass tubes.

Once in the hall your play began again,
Stopping only to have me move the band-aid
From your thumb to the back of your hand.
You liked band-aids, but only on the back of your hand,
No matter where the hurt.

Then the chemotherapy.
I held you down, while one nurse steadied the limb the I.V.
    was to go in.
Another nurse inserted the butterfly needle.
How you struggled!
I kept talking to you, saying over and over,
"It's okay, Eli. It's okay.
Mommy's here. It's okay.
Go ahead and scream son.
But please lie still."
When they were sure the needle was in a vein,
The doctor injected the drugs.
How I prayed during the process –
That they would find a vein easily,
That once in the needle would not slip out.

Then it was over.
It would take me several minutes to calm you down.
But soon we were in the car.
And this time I could share with you the excitement of the
    journey:
The journey home.

                        October 24, 1978

Halloween

I sewed patches on a shirt and an old pair of jeans.
After dressing you, I tried to smudge your face with ashes
      from the fireplace.
You fought that.
You didn't understand what was happening.

We slung a bag over your shoulder, and out you went with
      Daddy.
After an hour you were back.
And did you enjoy yourself!
You still weren't sure what was happening,
But the mystery, the excitement had filled you with happiness.

                    October 19, 1978

Santa Claus Parade

Daddy had dropped us off downtown.
We went into a store to buy you a pair of mitts;
While there we shared some fries and a coke.

We crossed the street, and I got you in position on my
    shoulders just as the parade was coming.
Even if I couldn't hear, I would have known when each band
    was approaching,
As you gently beat out their rhythm on my head with your
    hands.
Most of the parade I only saw through slits in the crowd.
You saw it all from your vantage point.
But even your Dad had no problem guessing what part you
    liked best.
From then on, parade was one of your favourite family games.

We would help you slip your head and an arm through the
    rope of one of the tabla drums,
Pad your shoulder with a towel, so the rope would not cut,
And then we were off,
You leading us around through the kitchen, the diningroom
    and the livingroom.
You'd be hitting your drum, Daddy and I in step behind,
    pretending we were playing horns.
At times you had us march in place, or turn tight circles,
But mostly we'd march in one large circle through the rooms.

Daddy and I always tired first; our imaginations were much
    more limited than yours.
For you the enjoyment of the Santa Claus parade did not just
    occur that one day;
But every time you could get Daddy and I to be young again,
    and with you form our own parade.

                                              January 4, 1979

Christmas Eve

We had bought you a wagon for Christmas.
It had to be assembled;
So that task we tackled Christmas Eve.

I remember planning a half hour to assemble your wagon.
Then we would sit in front of a roaring fire eating pop-corn.

Well, the half hour was expanding into two hours.
It was past ten; you weren't in bed,
And we had yet to pack to leave for London in the morning.
I was angry, I was tired, there was still so much to do.

Then I looked at you.
You were at your happiest.
For you were 'helping' your Dad put together your wagon.

I had to smile at myself.
What I had wanted was a quiet time together as a family,
      Christmas Eve.
I had it and almost missed noticing.

                                      December 13, 1978

Christmas Day

I can't remember who awoke first.
We were just as excited as Eli.
Eli's wagon was there by his bed,
Where he had insisted that it be left the night before.

Downstairs we opened the gifts.
Eli was so excited,
Especially with the big yellow car from his great-grandparents.

At church I remember Eli standing on the chair beside me,
Helping me hold the hymnal and singing so enthusiastically
That several times, when a song had ended, we had to bring it
    to his attention.

We had Jaya dedicated during the service.
Eli did not know what that was all about,
But he felt anything that included the rest of his family
    included him,
So he insisted on going forward with us.

At Gramma's and Papa's there were more gifts, more
    festivities,
As aunts, uncles and cousins were all present.
Eli was so full of energy, of joy,
That when his cousin Sarah, tired from all her celebrating,
    laid down on the living-room floor,
Her mother laughingly remarked, "You wouldn't know it was
    Eli who'd been so ill."

As we gathered for our family Christmas dinner,
Gramma said grace, thanking God that we were all together
    this Christmas time.

                                      January 1, 1979

Walk

It was a beautiful early winter's eve,
Sky clear, air crisp, snow white and deep,
Beautiful enough to draw me out of my lethargy.
"Come on, Eli. Do you want to go for a walk with Mommy?"

It was an enchanting evening.
Even Eli's redundant way of walking, forward ten feet, back
    eight,
Didn't irritate me.
I seemed to be caught up in his awe.

The wonder of snow,
The way it crunched underfoot, the way it moved when you
    kicked it,
The way it yielded to a stick as you poked it or moved the
    stick through it.

Returning by the river the magic increased.
As eternity seemed to be trapped in those moments together,
I was filled with a calm peace,
A gentle, tender love for Eli overflowing.

                                      August 24, 1978

Bed-Time Ritual

We'd usually put you to bed about eight.
You had to have your "hot bottle" at your feet,
Your blanket over you, then the other blankets,
Your favourite trucks and cars beside you.

Even in the spring this ritual couldn't be altered.
You still insisted on having a hot water bottle.

Then it was prayers.
The length of your prayer was a barometer of how tired you
    were.
The nights that you thanked God for each individual cousin,
    aunt, uncle, grandparent and playmate,
We knew that it would be an hour before you'd finish playing
    with your cars and trucks and drift off to sleep.

After prayers, we'd kiss you.
Then after blowing kisses from the door we'd go downstairs.

The longer your prayer the more frequently would be heard,
"Mom, come'ere."
I'd go up – usually some car or truck had fallen on the floor or
    got its wheels stuck.
At times I'd get exasperated with these interruptions.
But, what then was a nuisance,
Is now part of the warm memories of your bed-time ritual.

                              April 9, 1979

Good Times

For eight months you remained in remission, enjoyed good
    health.
We had a normal family life.
Watching you play and grow was a joy.

Many memories were created in that time:
You cranking up the swingomatic for your sister;
You 'fixing' the play-pen with your toy screwdriver and
    hammer;
The swim and craft session we took at the Y.
The frustrations of trying to toilet train you.

These were good times.
You seemed to have forgotten your pain and suffering,
And we too forgot not only the past but the future.

                                      September 9, 1979

Home

We came home in a cab.
We had not expected you to be discharged so soon.
"Stomach flu" had led to dehydration,
Which had led to three days in the hospital.

You seemed to share my great feeling of release, of joy.
As soon as we were home, you were on your tricycle,
Bombing around the basement.
Soon you had us playing one of our favourite family games,
Keeping Jaya, in her walker, out of the laundry room.
How we all laughed.

You soon tired,
But rested well that afternoon.
Papa and Grandma came.
You sat with your Daddy and watched Papa put up your
    swing-set.

At supper, Papa put your coke in a wine glass.
You liked that.
The mood was light, happy.
Papa told an action joke.
You laughed as loudly as any of us.
Then, we watched in amusement, as you repeated the actions
    of the joke.
You did not understand the joke,
But you understood the happiness.

I do not understand your death,
But I do understand the happiness your life brought to us.

                          October 5, 1978

Denial

Looking back I can see that the first evidence of the cancer's
    return was your voice change.
I first noticed it the day after what turned out to be your last
    chemotherapy treatment.
We hadn't given you anything for the nausea, and you'd been
    sick.
I thought that you were playing for sympathy,
So I said, "Eli, don't speak in a little boy's voice, you're a big
    boy."
Of course when your voice didn't improve there were other
    explanations:
A cold, allergies.

Then you awoke with a very painful neck.
You slept a lot.
Again, it could all be explained: your resistance was down
    because of the chemo.
You got better.

Then came the gastro-intestinal infection resulting in
    dehydration and a few days in hospital.
We'd just have to delay the chemo, get you built back up.

Then your appetite was off.
You became more moody.
You laid down more.
Well you needed to be built up.

Not feeling well, you did not like me leaving you, three half
    days to go to work.
No problem, I'd just take a leave of absence.

Every time you smiled or laughed,
Even though this was happening less and less,
We felt you were getting better.

We had been in close contact with your pediatrician all along,
But finally I took you back to Kitchener to see the cancer
    specialist.
He was shocked by your appearance.
He easily located the tumour in your abdomen.
He also felt that the change in your voice and your increasing
    difficulty in eating
Were due to another tumour in your chest.

He held out no hope!
He prescribed heavy pain-killing drugs and contacted your
    pediatrician.

We had known from the beginning that your type of cancer
    had only one remission.
Maybe that's why we delayed going back to the cancer
    specialist.
But even with our fears confirmed,
Did we really, could we really grasp, the meaning?

                                    September 8, 1979

Hypnotized

By the time it was confirmed the cancer was back,
Eli could no longer eat solids.
He could barely walk; after another week he never walked again.
And he was having trouble both passing urine and having a bowel movement.

Within a week a set routine was established.
Monday through Wednesday morning we would have a homemaker.
Thursdays and Fridays Grandma would be with us,
Weekends and evenings his Daddy.

We slept on the floor in the living room with him.
If he needed us we could quickly respond.
First thing in the morning when he awoke we would give him the pain medication.

Shortly thereafter I would have to begin giving him fluids.
This was a slow tedious process, often taking over half an hour for him to consume 2-3 oz.
I tried to make it easier by reading Christopher Robin poems to him in between sips.
Too often our efforts would seem almost in vain as fluid and mucous would roll out of his mouth.
It was not that he really coughed it up or even vomited; it just seemed to roll out.

He rested awhile,
And then we would go for a walk.
Daddy, Grandma or the homemaker pushed Jaya.
I pushed Eli, propped up in the baby carriage with his blanket covering him.

Back home if he had not urinated I would have to cradle him in a warm bath to encourage his water to come.
Then he would hardly have any rest before it would be time for him to have some more fluids.
While we got and had our lunch, I would lay him in front of the kitchen door so he could see us.

The afternoon was again punctuated with several feedings.
When the routine demanded nothing of us, I would sit beside him.
Often he wanted me to read.
Once I remember that he had his eyes closed; thinking he had gone to sleep, I stopped.
He opened his eyes immediately.
I said, "Eli, do you want Mommy to keep reading."
He nodded yes.
Then closed his eyes as I again began to read.

In the evening with Daddy home, we would go out in the backyard,
Or for a drive in the car.
But again he had to have several feedings,
Again another "bath" if he had not been able to urinate.

The routine demanded all our waking hours, all our energy.
Yet we needed that routine as much as he did.
We needed to give some physical expression to our love for him.

At the end of a day, when he had been able to take at least 14 oz. of fluid,
When he had been able to urinate on his own,
We felt good.
We thought maybe things are turning around; maybe things are beginning to get better.

Hypnotized by the routine, by the inability of our love to conceive of Eli's death,
The two most surprised, the two most shocked people when he died were his Daddy and Mommy!

Spring, 1979

Eyes

You had beautiful eyes,
So expressive, so alive.
They danced with the excitement of life.

But during those last few weeks
Your pain and suffering slowly drowned their light.
At times you were so weak
Your eyes would not even close in sleep,
Or awake they would drift uncontrollably toward the back of
      your head.

How it hurt to watch this,
This extinguishing of a candle.

I remember several times
A blank empty stare.
It frightened me!
I called to you!
I had to bring you back to this reality, to us!

Your last night
You were looking up,
Your father thought at me,
But your gaze was higher.
Were you even then preparing to leave?

                              August 9, 1978

Wasted

The weight seemed to fall off the arms and chest first;
The shoulders became thinner than the wrists.
Then changing a diaper one day I noticed
The loose folds of skin around the buttocks;
No longer did muscle and fat give them contour.

Looking through a magazine I stopped at a picture of a
        starving child:
Skin stretched over bone,
Abdomen swollen,
Eyes glazed.
And I cried.
For I realized it was you.

                          August 16, 1978

Words

For the last three weeks we slept with you in the living-room
    on the floor.
It was cooler than up in the bedrooms.
As well, being with you we were able to sense when you
    needed us.

I remember evenings lying on the floor beside you waiting for
    your Daddy to come to bed.
I would talk to you,
About life – what we had hoped it would be for you –
How life could be beautiful,
That it was worth the struggle.

Thinking back it was as if
I was half apologizing for what was happening to you,
Half encouraging you to keep fighting.
What I said would have seemed crazy to anyone listening in.
Here you were not yet three,
And I was rambling on with words and ideas it would have
    taken an adult to grasp.

But those were words I needed to say,
Words I needed to say to you, my child.

                                  January 7, 1979

Your Spirit

During the last two months you increasingly withdrew.
At times a quiet anger or a great sadness seemed to envelop
    you.
There were certain toys you would let no one touch.
Nor could anyone touch the glass of pop that you kept near
    you those last few weeks.
You began rejecting people,
Until only your Daddy and I could do anything for you.

About the middle of this time, I remember
You with a kleenex in one hand and one of Papa's candies in
    the other.
"What are you doing, Eli?" I asked.
"Jaya," you replied, as you knelt down,
To wipe the spit-up milk from your baby sister's mouth and
    then gave her the candy.

Another time, just a few days before you died, I remember
Your little friend Katie and her Mom visiting.
You were so tired you hardly seemed to notice them.
I offered Katie a drink of pop.
You started pointing at your glass.
I said, "Eli, do you want a drink?"
You shook your head, no.
"Do you want Katie to have some of your pop?"
You nodded, yes.
So I went and got another glass and poured some of your pop
    into it.
You were upset.
You turned onto your stomach and struggled to get up on your
    hands and knees.
"Eli, what's the matter?"
You pointed at your glass again.
"Eli, do you want Katie to drink out of your glass?"
You nodded, yes.

Twice your spirit shone through its prison of pain.

                                    September 19, 1978

In the Garden

Your Daddy had gone to his Wednesday evening group
 meeting.
I had finished the dishes.
Jaya was in bed.

I had planned, as usual, to take you into the garden.
But when I looked at you,
You had your eyes closed, so tired, so thin.
I could feel an anger growing in me.
I was beginning to understand how one could come to believe
 there was no God.
I was restless.
I needed to talk to someone,
But there was no one.

Mainly to burn off the energy of my restlessness
I decided to take you out into the garden.
I placed the chaise lounge in the shade.
I came back in.
"Come on son, Mommy is going to take you outside."

Once I got you settled with your pillow and blanket,
I was surprised to see how your eyes seemed to come alive.
You barely moved, but somehow you seemed
To be drinking in the freshness of the breeze, the songs of the
 birds.
My anger began to ease.
I started weeding the vegetable garden.

When I checked to see how you were
I was surprised to see mucous rolling out of your mouth, a
 mosquito resting unmolested on your nose
Before, you had always called me to help you with the mucous,
Had brushed away the mosquito yourself.
Now you seemed oblivious to both.
I cleaned you up,
And said, "Eli, call Mommy when you need her,"
But when I checked back you were in the same state.

The deep sadness that now enveloped me drowned what
    remained of my anger.
For I realized that you had become too weak to brush away
    the mosquitoes,
Too weak even to call me.

January 9, 1979

The War Was Over

I mixed fresh strawberries with the Sustenex.
You refused to take any.
And didn't I try.
Didn't I make a scene.
Then, I tried the Sustenex straight.
Still you refused.
Was I ever hot!
You were so weak, so thin.
You must take it!
It would give you strength, give you life.
But no.
Finally, I gave in, but not graciously.
I gave you apple juice,
But I let you know that I damn well wasn't pleased.

Later, I cooled down.
I remembered being told how stale the mouth became,
Making everything taste terrible.
I had tasted Sustenex –
Not your most appetizing drink at the best of times.

I went and sat with you.
I held your hand.
"Eli," I said,
"Mommy was wrong. I shouldn't have gotten angry.
Sometimes parents do stupid things.
I'm sorry."

You seemed to understand me.
Did you also understand,
What I had to deny?
The war was over.
All that remained was a dignified surrender,
And that in less than twenty-four hours.

September 12, 1978

Help Me

"Help me!" my son implored,
In a strained voice.
His lungs rattled with their fullness.
As he laboured to breathe,
I could hear the air moving through the secretions.

My calls awoke Willie.
We tried to suction him.
No way.
He hated suctioning,
And he summoned all his remaining strength to fight it.
Seeing this we stopped our efforts.
For this I'm thankful.
We sensed the need to respect his wish,
To respect his dignity.

Willie sat on a chair in the kitchen,
Alternately lying Eli prone over his knees or over his shoulder.
Like a rag doll Eli's limbs dangled loosely.
Dark brown filth leaked from his mouth.
I cleaned the floor where it fell,
Cleaned Eli's mouth,
Moved clean toweling under his head.

I became restless.
I put a finger in his limp hand.
Weakly he held it.
I whispered in his ear, "I love you."
I went to get a clean diaper.

Re-entering the kitchen I could hear Willie shouting, "Eli!
    Eli!"
Willie was squeezing Eli's chest,
A chest that refused to move.
Eli's eyes were half closed.
A brown stain ran from the corner of his mouth down his chin.
I hollered for Mom to come down.
Willie placed Eli on the chaise lounge that had been his bed
    the past two nights.

I knelt beside my son's body.
I held his hand that would never again close on mine.
I muttered, "It's okay, Eli."
But oh God, this time it isn't okay.
It hurt, how it hurt
Oh God, help me!

        August 8, 1978

The Observer at the Funeral

It was a beautiful day.
We arrived earlier than we had wanted:
So Willie and I went for a walk, hand in hand.
My body still filled with an energy that needed to be spent.

Returning I noticed the family, the friends who had come.
I was gratified by this show of concern.
I also was very aware of myself,
It was as if I was standing outside myself,
Observing what was happening.
It was Eli's funeral.
I knew it, and yet I felt detached.

After the service the pall bearers stood to move the coffin to
    the hearse.
The detachment threatened to break-down.
But soon the observer was back in control.

Leaving the grave-side,
I looked back at Eli's coffin, suspended above the hole.
Floral tributes were strewn over the mound of earth that
    would fall in behind the coffin.
I thought of the Saturday before,
When outside the variety store Eli had said, "Pop, Daddy,
    pop."
The two scenes didn't belong to the same reality.

At home I noticed myself smiling and talking with friends of
    my parents.
I remember our neighbour's Catalpa tree in full bloom,
Their daughter bringing me several of the blossoms,
Beautiful like orchids.
All this I remember and more.
And yet are these my memories or the observer's?

                              May 9, 1979

Nothing Worse

I used to think that there was nothing worse
Than a whining, screaming child:
Until I had a child
Who would whine and scream no more.

September 6, 1978

Out of the Garden

I had known pain and suffering were in this world,
But how superficial that knowledge was!
Then my son died.

All his previous pain and suffering had been acceptable,
For they had ended in remission.
But this time the ending was death.
For the first time I was called to fully comprehend the price of
    love.
And what a price!

I do not want to pay it.
I want my innocence back.
I want back into the Garden.
Reality is too cruel;
It's too painful.

But wait!
The one thing that I would not surrender to get back into the
    Garden,
Is having known Eli.

September 5, 1978

Your Blanket

We had them put your blanket in your coffin.
It seemed right.
The blanket had been your refuge throughout your life,
Whether you were sick or well.

I remember the time it got lost in the hospital laundry.
They said there was little chance we'd get it back.
About a week later you and your Daddy went to the laundry
    room to look for it.
You spotted it first.
It was yours all right.
Your name could still be faintly seen where grandma had
    written it.

You had your favourite cars, trucks and other toys,
Your favourite clothes, shoes.
But these favourites would change from time to time.
Your blanket was another thing – that never changed.
The wear and tear it showed witnessed to that.

How could we have kept your blanket?
It spoke so much of you.
It could so easily become a sacred relic.
So, we buried it with you.

We have no one thing that speaks to us of you.
And yet because we have no one thing, everything speaks to
    us:
The change of seasons, music, the laughter of children.
Making no one thing sacred you have made everything sacred.

                        April 2, 1979

Dreams

I dreamed about you again last night.
A variation of the same theme,
You were dead and yet alive.
We spent the day together, Jaya, you and I.
I took pictures.
Taking them I knew it was to prove that we had been together.
And yet the very fact that I had to prove anything showed
    that I knew you were dead,
That I knew it was a dream.

Probably the dreams would be interpreted as a form of denial.
A failure to fully accept your death.
Even the fact that most of my writings are addressed to you,
Would likely be seen as further evidence of this denial.

You are dead.
Intellectually I can accept that.
But my love for you did not die with you.
If anything it became more alive.
I became more acutely aware of its intensity, its depth.
You are dead.
My head can grasp that fact,
But can my heart?

                              May 1, 1979

Nothing Changed but Nothing was the Same

I used to feel that if I couldn't change what was happening,
That I could do nothing,
Or what I did really didn't matter.
Since nothing changed, my actions were impotent.

The strength and courage we were able to draw from
The many ways family, friends and co-workers
Reached out to help us, to let us know that they cared,
During Eli's illness, at the time of his death and since then,
Has convinced me differently.

Nothing changed – he died.
As much as they wanted, their help, their caring didn't change that.
But nothing was the same – their help, their caring did ensure that.
So although nothing was changed, nothing was the same.

                                          September 8, 1979

The Work of Grief

The work of grief is not to forget,
But to accept.

To accept that when asked about my family,
I can no longer mention you,
But must quieten my heart that cries,
"And there is Eli, there is Eli."

To accept that I can no longer hold you, talk with you,
That I will not know the heart aches and the joys of your
      growing into manhood,
That to our other children you will be little more than a name.

But despite this pain the work of grief is not to forget,
But to accept.

To accept most of all your last gift to me,
The gift of what I can learn by working through my grief.

"Because you are at the root of my life, because you once came into my life, my world is so full of joy, my life is filled with nectar."

Rabindranath Tagore

The Gift

It has been nearly a year since you died.
This past year has been hard without you,
Trying to piece together what happened.
Your death shook up my whole world,
My beliefs, my goals, my way of relating to others.

From the beginning I was aware
That a part of me had died with you,
And yet that I was richer for having known you.
It was mid-winter before I realized that the part of me that
      had died
Was my fear of living.

I had always known living could be risky, could be painful.
I had watched others being hurt.
Fearful of their pain, I protected myself well.

But you have taught me that although living can be risky, can
      be painful,
Life is not to be feared.
Losing you has hurt very much.
Yet how poor I would be if you had not been a part of my life.

Just under four years ago I gave you life.
In just as real a way,
You have given me life.

                                                   June 28, 1979

For I am convinced that neither death nor life,
neither angels nor demons,
neither the present nor the future,
nor any powers, neither height nor depth,
neither anything else in all creation,
will be able to separate us from the love of God
that is in Christ Jesus our Lord.
    Romans 8: 38, 39 (NIV)

About the Author

Kathleen James lives in Guelph, Ontario where she works as a physiotherapist and manual practice osteopath. She is a mother of four grown children and a grandmother of an ever growing number of grandchildren. Her husband, Willie, died in 2007.

www.ingramcontent.com/pod-product-compliance
Lightning Source LLC
Chambersburg PA
CBHW031206090426
42736CB00009B/804